The Fussy Puppy

By Cameron Macintosh

This is my puppy, Scruffy!

I love her a lot.

Scruffy is a happy puppy.

She loves to eat,
yet she is very fussy.

She munches on things
that are bad for dogs!

If Scruffy finds candy,
she bites it.

"Don't eat that, Scruffy!"
I say each time.

If some ice cream drips,
Scruffy licks it.

She's a typical puppy!

"Candy and ice cream are bad for dogs," said Mum. "That is not a myth!"

"We must find a safe snack for Scruffy," I said.

We got some safe snacks for Scruffy to try.

I hope she likes them!

Scruffy sniffed the melon,
but she did not bite it.

She looked away with a frown
on her face.

"Try this banana," I said.

Scruffy bit the banana,
but then she spat it out!

Scruffy did **not** like the banana.
She thought it was yucky.

"I will give this fussy puppy a turkey patty!" I yelled to Mum.

"Yes!" Mum yelled back to me. "Why not?"

I held a patty up to Scruffy's nose.

Scruffy sniffed the patty
and then chomped it!

She gave her tail a wag.

She seemed to say, "**Yum!**"

A turkey patty is a great safe snack for a fussy puppy!
She loves them!

CHECKING FOR MEANING

1. What snacks didn't Scruffy like? *(Literal)*
2. What safe snack did Scruffy like? *(Literal)*
3. How do you know that Scruffy didn't like the melon? *(Inferential)*
4. Do you think the narrator chose the right snacks for Scruffy to try? Why? *(Evaluative)*

EXTENDING VOCABULARY

typical	What does the word *typical* mean? In what ways was Scruffy a typical puppy? What would you do on a typical day?
myth	Is a myth something that is true or something that is made up? Can you think of a famous myth?
yelled	Look at the word *yelled*. What sounds are in this word? What is the base? What other word or words could the author have used instead of *yelled* in the text?

MOVING BEYOND THE TEXT

1. What does it mean to be fussy? Are you fussy about anything?
2. Do you think it would be fun to search for a new snack? Are there any foods that you would like to try?
3. What is your favourite healthy snack?
4. How can people take good care of a puppy?

TIME TO WRITE

Imagine you are Scruffy. Write a couple of sentences describing your typical day. Make sure you include what you do and what you eat.